Lucky Sussex

John Behague

Featuring records and photographs
from the H.S. Toms Archive of Flint and Folklore,
Booth Museum of Natural History,
the Royal Pavilion Libraries and Museums,
Brighton and Hove Council.

POMEGRANATE · PRESS

For Madeline
without whom
nothing would
have been
possible

Copyright © John Behague
Published in 1998 by Pomegranate Press,
Church Cottage, Westmeston, Sussex BN6 8RH

Cover Design: David Marl

ISBN 0 9519876 5 8

British Library Cataloguing-in-Publication Data.
A catalogue record of this book is available from the British Library.

Printed by Island Press, 3 Cradle Hill Industrial Estate,
Seaford, East Sussex, BN25 3JE.
Telephone 01323 490222

Contents

———————————

The Magic of Sussex

This is a place full of magic,
As wondrous a spot as you'll find,
Where luck is as likely to bless you
As love for its vistas so wide.

About the author

John Behague is a former newspaper editor and broadcaster, who was for several years programme organiser of BBC Radio Brighton. He is widely travelled and has visited many remote and exotic places. Sussex, however, is his choice as the best of them in which to live and work, as he has done happily for the past 30 years.

Acknowledgements and thanks

My thanks to Madeline, my principal proof reader, advisor, finder and minder; David Arscott for his help, trust, and encouragement; John Cooper, Keeper of the Booth Museum, for opening doors and files and putting me on the right track; Dr. Fatimah Lateef for her valuable digging; Ian Wells for providing the old prints; and Graham Pritchard, photographer and Magic Circle member, for pictures which came and went.

The photographs in the H.S. Toms chapter were supplied by the Royal Pavilion, Libraries and Museums, who hold the copyright.

Book list

Some of the books quoted in these pages are, alas, out of print, and you may have to scour the secondhand bookshops to find copies, but they are well worth searching for.

Flint. Its Origin, Properties & Uses, by Walter Shepherd (Faber).
The Pebbles On the Beach, by Clarence Ellis (Faber).
By the Crown Divided, by Cecile Woodford (Crown Quality Books).
Tales of Old Sussex, by Lillian Candlin (Countryside Books).
Memories of Old Sussex, by Lillian Candlin (Countryside Books).
A Sussex Garland, by Tony Wales (Godfrey Cave Associates).
Sussex - Customs, Curiosities, Country Lore, by Tony Wales (Ensign).
The Green Roof of Sussex, by Charles Moore (Middleton Press).
Smugglers' Village, by Henry Blyth (H.E. Blyth Ltd.).
Along the South Downs, by David Harrison (Cassell).

Luck, logic and the power of the mind

A billion years of pounding tides,
Untold creatures fossilised.
Silica, sand and chalk combine
In alchemy that baffles mind.
Scorching sun, primaeval muck
All contribute to our luck!

Y ou may think it odd that a journalist trained to deal with facts and figures should want to write a book about luck. Perhaps I should explain, then, that for the best part of my life I have been fascinated by the unexplained and unfathomable, the stories that lead you into both shiny and dark corners, the contradictions of life and the remarkable world of coincidences. I have found some subjects surrounded by almost impenetrable barriers, some studded with taboos, and areas no self-respecting writer should enter if he wishes to avoid being labelled a crank.

When I worked in the main newsroom of the BBC in London these restrictions were all too apparent, and stories were regularly ditched because they were considered 'too way out' or 'not on'. That is not to say that other departments did not depart from the norm and carry out serious investigations into every subject under the sun, but they were not subject to the same unwritten rules.

At one time an effort was made to end news bulletins and programmes with what were called 'tail enders'. These were entertaining little stories of strange or amusing events, and listeners looked forward to hearing them. You seldom get such departures these days. There was also a man named Jack deManio who presented the equivalent of the *Today* programme. He often got the time wrong but he had a liking for happy endings and good luck stories that endeared him to his followers and made him something of a national institution. He didn't last long enough to draw a full pension, and went into public relations, like so many other outcasts.

The trouble with professional newsmen and women is that they become steeped in the hard stuff and blinkered by prejudice, so that they miss out on some really good human interest stories. They're a gloomy lot today.

I was lucky (yes, it's that word again) during my last few years with the BBC. I took over the training of its journalists, and I had as my motto IPTBI - It Pays To Be Inquisitive. I tried to instil in my students the need to look beyond the headlines into causes and effects. When I retired and set up my own training courses in Sussex I was able to point the way into other worlds and philosophies, and I used the methods of Dr. Edward de Bono, of Lateral Thinking fame, to help me achieve this.

Encounters with the unusual

Sussex is so full of incredible places and people as to provide material for any number of books and articles. Incredible? Magicians and white witches abound. A nuclear engineer friend who lived in Sussex had the most alarming experiences with poltergeists. Some respected members of the community admit to being dowsers, and I have had my own encounters with the unusual and unaccountable in Brighton.

As for luck, lucky stones and wishing heads, surely, you may say, it's all superstitious twaddle. There's nothing to it. It's all in the mind. There's no doubt that much of it *is* in the mind, and that thinking does make things so. 'As a man thinketh in his mind and in his heart so is he.' There's ample evidence to prove that our grey matter is all-powerful, and by using it to strong purpose we can make our own luck. It's called positive thinking, and many successful people today practise it.

In the case of the Rottingdean wishing stone, those people who work themselves into a tizzy over it and challenge its supposed magic tend to invite misfortune. But the power lies within the mind and not the stone. There are some who would disagree with me on this, including T.C. Lethbridge, a distinguished archaeologist and researcher, who believed that inanimate objects like stones did possess some kind of energy, but that's another story.

They became precious objects

Lucky mascots and talismans remain popular. One of my grandaughters wouldn't go anywhere without her lucky rabbit. Some motorists have St. Christopher medallions permanently fixed to their dashboards. Theatrical folk are particularly taken up with lucky mascots. Elderly gentlemen still treasure their old teddy bears. During the war years RAF air crews carried lucky charms with them on every trip. It's all a matter of belief. It concentrates the mind. Any psychologist will tell you that the stronger the belief, the more likely you are to reach your goal. In the words of the old song 'Wishing will make it so!'

In olden days in Sussex the holed stones people carried in their pockets or around their necks became more precious than any other items or adornments. They were more than guardians against the Devil: they had their medical properties, too. Rubbed against aching joints or fevered brows they brought temporary relief.

Superstitions, in the light of today, may appear silly, but when they were written some served to warn, guard or advise people about such things as the weather, agriculture, ambition, cookery and coping with everyday living. Many sayings are now lost in antiquity, of course, but some still serve a useful purpose.

There would be room for a book solely on the many hundreds of superstitions, talismans and potions surrounding love. The young single women of today may not follow the custom of their ancestors in picking up bunches of daisies and using them to forecast the date of their nuptials, or seeking the advice of a fortune teller for details of any tall, dark, handsome stranger. They are more inclined to put on their glad rags and go out and grab one!

In Sussex today, the gentle maiden has given way to a black leather-coated, crash-helmeted vision on a motor bike, determined to set a fast pace. Life used to be so peaceful and predictable in those misty old days of yore, when custom, civility and the family prevailed and luck seemed to have been around in larger lumps.

Stones with holes in them

Y ou may not realise it, but when you step out along the shingle beaches of Sussex you are walking on a remarkable inheritance. It is one which once played an important part in the lives of the local people, from the very earliest residents to those who lived here in Victorian times, but which today has been sadly neglected and for the most part forgotten.

How many people living on the 65-mile stretch of coast between Rye and Bognor Regis, I wonder, have ever heard of the Sussex lucky stones? Very few, it seems. As for the hundreds of thousands of holiday makers who flock down to the coast every year to swim, beachcomb and throw stones in the sea, how many, with feet crunching on the masses of pebbles, have ever paused to examine what lies around them?

The Devil's luck

Sussex people have always been at war with the devil. One dark night he tried to drown the place by digging a dyke to let in the sea, but was thwarted at the last moment by a bit of good luck. Someone lit a candle and he fled, thinking it was the dawn!

It was believed that when you dined, the Devil sat on your left shoulder and your guardian angel on the right. It was thought a bad omen if you spilt salt, but you could overcome this by throwing a pinch of it over your left shoulder into the eyes of the devil. Alas and alack, if you forgot and threw it over your right shoulder, the Devil would be mighty pleased.

Before we go any further, I have to tell you that there are two distinct and separate kinds of lucky stones, and they have been known by many different names over the years, including holey stones, hag stones, ague stones, witch stones, thunder stones and shepherds' crowns. The latter two are fossilised sea urchins (*see page 37*) and the others are flints with holes through them, but all come under the general heading of lucky stones.

These holed flints are there in their thousands. They may be hard to spot at first, but when you run your fingers through the shingle they begin to appear – large ones, small ones, some smooth, some rough and grotesquely shaped. Some look as if they have been finely bored with a diamond drill, some have large ragged holes you can poke a finger through.

Curative powers

They are the the stones which were once believed to possess magical and curative powers, and were thought to be exclusive to this one special shoreline in the world, and they still remain very much a mystery. So far as it is known, it is not possible to discover them in such large and exposed numbers in any other part of the country. They are there in Dorset, the Isle of Wight and other parts where there is a profusion of chalk. Flint occurs in East Yorkshire, too, but shingle banks do not form on the foreshore in the same way as on the south coast. Oddly enough, visitors to the beaches of Normandy, on the other side of the Channel, have found similar stones there, but not in the same quantity as in Sussex.

As I have said, the one strange and common feature of these puzzling pebbles is the hole or holes through the middle. In some cases there can be two or three holes, all perfectly formed, and it is when you consider the history of the stones that you begin to realise that the perforations must be the work of an intriguing force of nature.

When moggy meets magpie, fur will fly

Birds and cats figure prominently in Sussex superstitions. A very old one declares: 'When a black cat and a magpie meet, bad luck will come to the village street.'

Five thousand years is a long time back, yet there is evidence that the early settlers on the Sussex coast did collect such stones, and thought them important enough to want them placed in their graves – a custom which appears to have persisted until almost the present day, as we shall learn later. During excavations at neolithic sites in Brighton before the war, several skeletons were found, together with holed stones and shepherds' crowns.

They were members of the Windmill Hill culture, a tribe who were among the first potters in Britain, and some of their remains and relics are on display in Brighton Museum. The inscription says two young women, one with a baby, were found buried in ditches around Whitehawk camp. Two holed stones can be clearly seen beside them, together with a couple of fossilised sea urchins, although the inscription refers only to the latter.

Much later, when a small fishing town named Brighthelmstone appeared on the map, the locals held the stones in great respect. They regarded them as lucky talismans capable of warding off sickness and misfortune. The women threaded smaller pebbles together for wearing around the neck or wrist, and the men carried them in their pockets.

Countering the evil eye

In her book *Portrait of Sussex*, Cecile Woodford has described how her grandmother, a midwife and healer, had such faith in the stones that she would not venture out without a bagful to insure against possible accidents. She also used them for 'scraping off' diseases from sick children and protecting adults against contagion.

It was this rubbing of the stones against arthritic limbs or pains in the head or body that made them so popular. It was also believed that they helped to counter the evil eye, witches and the Devil.

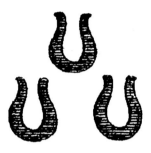

Keeping the Devil at bay

*The luck of the horseshoe has Sussex
origins. According to legend, St.
Dunstan, the Mayfield blacksmith who
became Archbishop of Canterbury in
960 AD, was tempted in his forge by the
Devil disguised as an alluring young
woman. Dunstan, spotting a tell-tale
pair of cloven hoofs, put his adversary
to flight by seizing his nose in his red-
hot tongs. Ever since that time a
horseshoe over the door has been a sure
way of keeping the Evil One at bay.*

Sussex farmers called them 'hag stones' and nailed them to their barn doors to protect the cattle. As further safeguards they hung up polished brasses and cross-shaped pieces of iron to deflect evil influences. Orchards were also protected by holed stones strung between the trees.

To make holed stones more potent in the treatment of sick people, the pebbles would be exposed to the full moon for three consecutive nights and then placed beneath the patient's mattress. They were used in the same way to ward off nightmares and bad dreams.

Superstition has it that any stone with a hole in the middle will bring good luck to the finder if worn around the neck or on a key chain. Seamen particularly valued them if they found them on the shore, and fishermen believed that to have them on board helped them in their catches. There was also a belief that if a holed stone were hung over the bed of a woman in labour it would make the birth much smoother.

Far bigger stones

The tradition of using holed stones for protection was not confined to Sussex. In some counties they were called 'ring stones' and were hung around the necks of farm animals. These should not be confused with the unique flint lucky stones. Far bigger stones with holes in them than are to be found on the beaches in Sussex have become famous for their healing powers. Near Madron, in Cornwall, there is a large stone with a hole through it about two feet in diameter. It is claimed that relief from a variety of illnesses can be obtained by crawling through the hole. Other similar stones in Ireland are said to prevent rickets in children and cure measles and other maladies.

There is a record of a large holed slab of rock in the middle of the river Dee which is said to promote fertility in barren women, and a stone at Hart in Cleveland which cures people who sit on it'. One suspects that the power of the mind is greater than that of the stone, but some of the cures are well documented.

Lucky pigs

One Sussex belief was that if you wished to be a successful pig farmer you had to love your animals and treat them with the respect intelligent creatures deserve.

It was considered unlucky to send any to slaughter during certain months. The saying was 'Unless your bacon you would mar, kill not your pigs in months lacking R.' This meant that during May, June, July and August porkers were safe from the butcher's knife. Since they used to be considered our warmest months, and pork doesn't keep very well in hot weather, it was probably a wise practice.

The big mystery

There remains the mystery of how the stones were holed in the first place. Some of those found along the Sussex coast contain perforations so fine as to be almost like pinholes, while other holes are much bigger. Some experts say that the smaller ones could be caused by marine organisms — minute worms, no more than half an inch long, whose bodies are covered with short bristles and whose heads bear tentacles which coil up like corkscrews. They attack most rocks and are thought to secrete a substance which eats into the stones and forms a soluble organic compound.

Larger holes could be the work of such molluscs as the wrinkled rock borer or red nose, which makes a funnel-shaped start to its operations. Other borers of large cylindrical holes include the little piddock, which possesses rasp-like teeth and is quite tenacious.

However, no worms or molluscs have been found capable of making an impression on flint, and since many of the holed pebbles found on Sussex beaches were originally flint nodules, science appeared to remain undecided. My researches remained in limbo until the middle of 1996, when a Singapore medico friend, Dr. Fatimah Lateef, arrived on the scene, found a lucky stone for herself, and became determined to fathom its secrets. The holey truth was hard to find, but she persisted and presented a heap of detailed notes which any geologist would have been proud to possess, but which made as much sense to me as a treatise on quantum physics.

The breakthrough came in mid-1997 when my wife Madeline and I met John Cooper at the Booth Museum in Brighton. Here was a geologist worth his rock-salt, a man surrounded by dinosaur bones, skeletons of killer whales and fossil fish hundreds of millions of years old. A man who not only had the ability to explain the complications of nature clearly and simply, but who was also the Keeper of the Lucky

Cuckoo conundrum

Hearing a cuckoo call was reckoned to bring good luck, but it depended on where you were at the time. If standing on grass, that was fine, and if you turned the money over in your pocket you could expect a lot more. Too bad, however, if you happened to be on barren ground. All you got was cuckoo spit! The money-making ritual also applied when viewing a new moon.

An old woman would let a cuckoo out of her bag at the Heffle (Heathfield) Fair each April 14 in order to launch the Spring - and if you heard the bird on that day it was a sign of great happiness to come.

Stone Archives, handed down by a former curator of Brighton Museum, H.S. Toms, from whom we shall learn more later. There was a delicious scent of discovery and decay in the air as we embarked on a trip into the farmost realms of the Earth's history.

John Cooper confessed that he didn't know all the answers, but what he did tell us made a great deal of sense. The first thing to realise, he said, is that holed stones are not unique to Sussex, and wherever you find chalky outcrops you can usually find flint. The chalk itself formed as a muddy ooze on the floor of a deep, clear sea which covered much of Northern Europe between 100 and 65 million years ago. Composed of the remains of microscopic shelly plankton, the ooze slowly accumulated and consolidated, entombing the shells and skeletons of a myriad sea creatures. Commonest among them were the remains of the siliceous or glass sponges, simple forms of animal life.

Sponges and silica

Over time, the bodies of these sponges gave up their silica through dissolution, only for it to be redeposited around decaying organic debris as the material we now know as flint. As the flint formed and hardened, it sometimes preserved as fossils the shapes of seashells, crabs, starfish and other creatures as well as many of their burrows and borings. In filling the latter the growing flint frequently enclosed a small portion of sea floor which was not turned to flint. And there you have it – the origin of a holed flint – your actual lucky stones. There was no way that holes could have developed *after* the flints were formed.

During the 19th century, John said, various so-called experts and amateur geologists wrote supposedly learned pamphlets about flint stones, connecting their weird shapes with objects like gourds, tree roots and branches, human fingers, hands, feet and other animal bits and pieces. Bizarre! Now we know much more, said John. After our visit to the Booth Museum, with its rich collection of minerals, fossils and glass sponges, we certainly do.

Fishy rituals

Sussex fishermen are not much different from those elsewhere in the British Isles. They all tend to be superstitious. Very few, alas, are now left, but a century ago, when fishing was a major industry in Sussex, many different customs were followed to bring good luck and appease the gods.

Lucky stones were the first objects of defence, and were easy enough to find, but there were certain rules to obey if you wished to bring home a good catch. Fishermen had a private language and some everyday words were banned. Friday was thought to be an unlucky day and one in which to stay at home and repair the nets. Superstitions die hard, and I am told that even today some yacht owners in Sussex refuse to set sail on a Friday.

Among the items in the museum's collection of lucky stones is one bearing the following inscription:

'This lucky stone was presented to W.G.J. Jacobs by H.S. Toms Esq. The greatest gift to cure all ills.'

Who W.G.J. Jacobs was, we may never know, but was the present meant as a joke, or was the workaholic curator of the Brighton Museum serious about its healing effects?

It should be added that of the several theories unearthed by Dr. Lateef most related to the chemical processes at work within the Earth's chalky deposits. The starting or initiating point was thought to be a sponge centre, around which chalk and silica were deposited. With time, decay of the flesh of the dead sponge produced ammonia. The central region thus became hollow, creating the hole, and the ammonia acted as a stimulus to further deposition of silica to complete the flint stone. That is a simplification of a long, technical explanation of one theory. John Cooper is probably much nearer the mark, though even he agrees that the chemistry of flint formation is complex, and barely understood.

So, what made them so attractive to those early settlers in Sussex five or six thousand years ago, as they huddled in their caves near the sea? The stones must have been seen as something special – objects to be examined and handled with respect. Perhaps they were even venerated, since some chose to be buried with the holed flints. Then, as life in Sussex progressed, more and more claims were made for them.

No fisherman would venture to sea without a handful of lucky stones aboard. It was thought they would protect against the winds and waves and help bring in a good catch. When I spoke to one of the few remaining old fishermen left in Brighton a few years ago, he took me to his small, well weathered boat and showed me his collection. He still wouldn't go to sea without them, he said.

Defy the Devil with garlic

Garlic has been hailed as a finer remedy for good luck and good health than any other plant. People have been taking it for ages in Sussex, and there is a thriving garlic centre at Catsfield, near Battle in East Sussex. In the olden days it was thought to be effective in warding off the Devil's advances. Today there is mounting scientific evidence of its efficacy in preventing colds and lowering blood pressure.

In her book *Memories of Old Sussex*, Lillian Candlin wrote of the pleasures of hunting for lucky stones on Brighton beach when she was a child. The tradition, she said, was to give a good spit through the hole and then throw the stone over the left shoulder. 'If there is no one sitting behind this will bring good luck!'

In Victorian days, as the stone went over the shoulder, the children chanted:

> *Lucky stone, lucky stone, bring me some luck*
> *Today or tomorrow at twelve o'clock.*

Another little ditty went:

> *Lucky stone, lucky, go over my head,*
> *and bring me some luck before I go to bed.*

Toms also mentions these rhymes in his notes, and Sir John Evans in his publication *Ancient Stone Implements* recalls the first little rhyme. He writes of the supposed power of the stones and of the belief in years gone by that they could protect cattle. In the museum at Leicester, he says, is a witch stone, a pebble with a natural hole, which was preserved for many generations in one family, and had great virtues attributed to it. 'It prevented the entrance of fairies into the dairy. It prevented milk from taint. It kept off diseases, charmed off warts and seems to have been valuable alike to man and beast.'

Half a century ago it was still possible to see lucky stones nailed to barn doors in Sussex. Not any more. The modern farmer has no time for superstition. He prefers to protect his crops and animals with electronic devices. Down on the beach no one bothers to pick them up, except for wave skimmers. But what a precious asset to the tourist trade they might provide if properly promoted.

Toms said what made lucky stones so popular was that they could be carried in your pocket, hung at the door to keep out witches or put at

Lucky apples

The apple tree has always been close to the hearts of the people of Sussex. Not only was it regarded as a symbol of fruitfulness but it played a particular role among girls seeking suitable sweethearts. A maiden would solemly peel an apple and then throw the cutting over her shoulders on to the ground. On careful inspection, and if she was very lucky, she would see the initial of her future husband.

To cut down an apple tree was said to be unlucky, and to leave a single apple on a tree at harvest time would, it was said, lead to a death in the family.

The saying 'An apple a day keeps the doctor away' is believed to come from an old myth in which apples were presented to the gods to stave off old age.

the head of your bed to cure ague. Placed on the window-sill (which he called the 'museum' of a cottage) they'd also keep out witches. On the stable door they'd prevent the entrance of witches, pixies and fairies 'who are apt to borrow a horse and ride it furiously all night so that the poor beast is very foam-flecked and tired in the morning!'

In addition to these uses, he discovered other places where they were considered essential. He told the story of a lifeboatman who wore one. When he was ill, the crew, who believed firmly in its efficacy to prevent drowning, refused to go to the rescue of a boat until he was brought down and carried on to the lifeboat on a stretcher. Then the rescue was safely made. Toms also mentioned that at one time all the fisherwomen in Brighton carried lucky stones.

He described a witch stone as an ordinary stone with a natural hole through it, and a shepherd's crown as a fossilised sea urchin. Both these potent charms were so ordinary as to be picked up frequently on the beach and on the hills, but they were not to be despised. They acted against illness and witches, he said, and brought good luck.

A fear of witches

A century ago in Sussex there seemed to be a genuine fear of witches. So many of Toms's notes refer to them, and he built up a photograph album of window-sills lined with batteries of stones placed there as a deterrent to the hags on horses and to Old Nick himself. The regard for the stones, he explained, dated from prehistoric times, and later the charms were discovered with Saxon and Roman burial remains. The lore remained constant for many years. He quoted the case of a Portslade woman who was buried with the stone she had worn all her life.

If you found a holed stone, you should spit on it for luck, wish, then throw it over your left shoulder. He reckoned that a whole lecture could be written on the folk lore of spitting. By spitting you sacrificed part of yourself and you paid homage to the god of love by throwing the object

Unlucky bird

*In the Dark Ages in Sussex, when the county
was regularly invaded by marauders, the
cock was considered an unlucky bird. When
the Danes had taken over the town of
Hastings and the locals were about to make
a surprise counter attack on the sleeping
occupiers, a treacherous cock crowed loudly
and woke them up, thus foiling the attempt.*

*So disgusted were the townspeople that they
created a Shrove Tuesday game called
cock-in-the-pot. It involved a live cock in a
clay pot at which sticks and stones were
hurled. The first to break the pot won the
bird.*

over the left shoulder. On the other hand, you could keep the stone and wear it round your neck for luck or to keep away illness. He said the custom had been very extensive and was common to most of England.

It may sound a tall story, but Toms insisted that in the early days of the motor car, visitors to Brighton used to find a lucky stone on the beach and tie it to the back axle of their vehicle to ensure a safe return journey. Today, I suppose, it might be effective in preventing a parking fine or getting you through a traffic jam, but I doubt it.

Another bit of lucky stone lore was to keep one in your house to make sure you never lacked bread.

Striking personality

The Brighton curator must have been in great demand for his talks and lectures in pre-war Sussex. He had a striking personality with his bushy moustache and elegant appearance. He knew how to keep an audience entertained, and his flow of words was clear and colourful. He was particularly appreciated when, at the end of a talk, he distributed lucky stones among his audience so that they could test their effectiveness for themselves.

He once said it might be ridiculed, but witches had certainly got powers, and there were still some witches living. Though ninety per cent of their power was accounted for by the power of suggestion, they had psychic gifts, which were real. He made that statement just sixty years ago, and witches are still with us today. White ones, that is, and they ride comfortably around in smart Ford coupes!

There is the story of the old Brighton lady who did quite a trade with summer visitors by selling necklaces made from the stones. She'd gather them in the winter months, clean, polish and thread them ready to offer from a large basket close to where the Chain Pier once stood. That was way back in the thirties, and no one has bothered to exploit

Swallow this

Swallows have always been thought lucky birds in Sussex. To have a swallow family living under the eaves of your house was said to be very fortunate indeed, as it would protect your property from lightning and storms.

According to folklore swallows are said to carry two precious stones within their bodies - a red one which can cure insanity and a black one which brings good luck.

them since. It seems strange that here we have an unlimited, free supply of a unique item but nobody willing to market it.

Stone startled a nation

My personal stories of lucky stones are many and varied. When travelling around I always carried one in my coat pocket. It helped to break the ice on social occasions and one day even startled an entire nation. When, as a visiting journalist, I was interviewed on national television in Jordan, the presenter grilled me about the lucky stone I'd earlier shown him. I was invited to hold it up in full view of the camera whilst he delivered a good humoured ribbing about the superstitious English. It went on a bit. The lights were bright and it was very hot. I began to feel perspiration on my brow and my arm was beginning to ache. Then quite suddenly and dramatically the stone shot at least two feet in the air from my fingers and hit the studio desk with a resounding crash.

There was a shocked look from the interviewer, followed by three or four seconds of awesome silence. I said: 'That's what happens when you insult a lucky stone!' He never really recovered from it, and quickly went on to another subject, but the reaction from the audience was enormous and for the rest of my stay in Jordan people rushed up to me begging to see 'the stone that jumps'. What they didn't realise was that there was nothing magical about it – finger pressure, perspiration and smooth flint did the trick. I've tried it several times since, but not on television.

In Holland, where I helped to train journalists from all parts of the globe, lucky stones formed part of my stock in trade, and entire radio features were made around them. There are Sussex lucky stones in Singapore, Zambia, Australia, The Gambia, South Africa, Canada, Nigeria, Qatar, Tanzania, China, Hong Kong, Malta, Malaysia, Fiji, Gibraltar, Tonga, Tuvalu, Nepal, India, Pakistan, Botswana, Brunei, Switzerland and Finland. How do I know? Because I taught students from each of those countries and brought them down to Brighton to

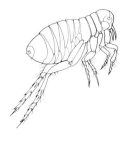

In a flap about fleas

March 1 was traditionally the day for ridding yourself of fleas in Sussex, although people went about it in different ways. In some areas they would shut their windows tight to prevent the horrible little creatures getting in, while in others they would fling their doors and windows open, crying 'Welcome, March!'

In Arundel there was a procession to the bridge, where local folk would shake themselves and their clothing - supposedly keeping themselves free of fleas for the rest of the year.

meet some of its personalities and – of course – to find their own lucky stones!

Before my Dutch Uncle act I trained radio and television journalists for the BBC at Broadcasting House in London and also ran international courses, the members of which enjoyed a trip down to Sussex. Towards the end of one course we were visited by the Director General, who had earlier spent a morning with the students.

'What,' he demanded of them, 'was the most rewarding moment of your course here?' They all looked at one another. I knew what he was thinking. The talk he'd given on accuracy and integrity must surely have left its mark. No one stirred. 'You there!' he gestured to a chap from Kuala Lumpur sitting at the back. 'Come on, tell us about the best thing you've gained from this course.'

Amin made his way to the front, and proceeded to take off his coat. I watched with some apprehension. He then took off his tie and slowly began to unbutton his shirt. The DG was now goggle-eyed. 'Good God, man!' he exclaimed. 'What on earth's going on?'

'Well, sir,' said my man from KL, 'you did ask what was the best thing I got from the course, and this is it,' and plunging his hand down his shirt front he produced a silver chain at the end of which was strung a highly polished pebble. 'It's a lucky stone, sir', said Amin, 'and John here helped me find it.'

The BBC's Head Man turned slightly purple. 'I'll see you later,' he told me, and departed somewhat hurriedly. For some reason, he never raised the matter again. Perhaps he'd decided it had all been an hallucination – or it could have been the power of the lucky stone that saved me from the chop.

It's when you take a broader look at holed stones that you realise the possibilities for exploitation they still hold, but there is a catch. According to legend any stones with holes in them will bring luck to

Blowing away the screws

Way back in the 18th century in Sussex, life was cold, damp and uncomfortable, and many people suffered with the screws, or rheumatism as it is more properly called. Doctors were ill-equipped to deal with it, but lucky nutmegs carried in a pocket were commonly used, as were pairs of bellows placed behind one's back when sitting on a chair.

The idea was that when you leaned forwards and backwards, the air from the bellows would blow away the pain. I much prefer the nutmeg approach, and despite the passing of the years and advancement of medical science, some people still do!

their finders, but you have to find them for yourself. So the act of selling or passing them on to others might mean that you rob them of their vital powers. Toms had his own theory about this, and loved to hand out stones as well as receive them.

A century ago holed stones must have been in great demand. A correspondent to a newspaper in 1851 wrote: 'I recently observed a large stone having a natural hole through it, suspended inside a farmer's cow house. Upon inquiring of a labourer, I was informed this was intended as a preventative of nightmare in the cattle. My informant (who evidently placed great faith in its efficacy), added that a similar stone suspended in a bedroom, or a knife or steel laid under the foot of the bed, was of equal service to the sleeper, and that he himself frequently made use of this charm.'

Hope of relief

Natural rock formations encompassing small holes are to be found in parts of Cornwall, the Grampians and County Waterford, and are visited by pilgrims and others in the hope of relief for their ailments. All very pagan, you may think, but when your bones begin to ache, your baby has croup once again, your back aches and there's no doctor for miles around, you'd be excused for having a go, even if the local priest had warned you against the work of the Devil. That certainly was the case in days of yore, and there is clear evidence that people are still using the old methods today.

Finding a husband

The stone dolmens of France and England are also claimed to possess healing powers, and to make delivery easier for pregnant women. There is an added attraction for some in that they can help young girls find husbands. That's another service you can't get on the NHS.

A photograph taken in 1891 of the beach in Brighton with the Chain Pier in the background. It may be hard to imagine, but all those sitting on the shingle were fully decked out in tight fitting clothes. There may have been plenty of lucky stones on view, but not a single bare knee.

My travelling days are now over, and I no longer carry lucky stones with me. They have, however, provided me with much pleasure over the years, and have helped to form many a friendship. I like to think that out there in Malaysia or high in the Himalayas there is a former student with a silver chain around his neck and a souvenir from Sussex hanging close to his heart.

Some call them shepherds' crowns, others thunder stones, and there are lots of other names on record, but most people prefer to call them lucky stones.

Shepherds' crowns and thunder stones

They were variously known as shepherds' crowns, thunder stones, ague stones, fairy crowns, fairy waves and policemen's hats, but they are all fossil sea urchins and were said to have the same powers as holed flint stones.

You will not find them in such abundant supplies as holed stones. The place to go a few years ago was Black Rock, the spot where they built Brighton Marina, but now you have to look elsewhere.

In a talk on shepherds' crowns in archaeology to Brighton Natural History Society, in January, 1940, H.S.Toms stressed the archaeological importance of various excavations at neolithic sites in which the fossil echinoderms or sea-urchins had been found buried with human interments.

These instances were not unique, he said. Shepherds' crowns had been found elsewhere in prehistoric Bronze Age and early Iron Age graves, together with arrow heads and pottery. Some had been discovered furnished with a metal loop for use as amulets, and when in folk lore they came to be called thunder stones, they were equally treasured.

It was believed that thunder stones fell from the sky during thunderstorms or whenever lightning struck. Crowns were regarded as thunder stones because of their rounded shape, similar to sling stones, the idea doubtless being that they were hurled to earth from the sling of the Thunder God.

Holed flint stones and shepherds' crowns are both regarded as being lucky, but they are quite different in appearance.

The stone was believed to protect a house against lightning, and in many parts was kept lying on a shelf, on a chest of drawers or in a box, or in a place where it might be free from disturbance. Sometimes it was laid under the floor, on the top of a four-poster bedstead, or under the roof.

The thunder stone was held to be efficacious in keeping pernicious creatures like witches away, and it also provided protection for houses and cattle. Some people carried thunder stones or shepherds' crowns in their pockets as a protection when out in a storm.

Mr. Toms on the trail

Early in 1933 Toms was told of a follower of the thunder stone lore living at Cocking in West Sussex, who had used shepherds' crowns as charms against lightning. The ever-keen curator of Brighton Museum was thus encouraged to investigate this Sussex backwater and in August of that year set out to discover how many shepherds' crowns had survived in the Cocking district. He obtained, he said, not only evidence of rare survival but interesting confirmation of crowns being placed on mantelpieces to prevent lightning strikes. Later he found evidence that in the twenties in several parts of Sussex, including Brighton, shepherds' crowns were spoken of as 'thunder bolts' or 'thunder stones'.

Toms said he'd found that, though the lore of shepherds' crowns must formerly have been widespread in the chalky districts of southern England, it was now rapidly disappearing. The lore had lived on persistently through the ages and had spread far and wide. With obvious regret, he had to report that the idea of luck attached to shepherds' crowns had vanished almost entirely from whole groups of Sussex villages during the past half century, after playing such a prominent part among country folk.

The man who broke the bank

One of the luckiest men ever to live in Sussex was Charles Wells, 'the man who broke the bank at Monte Carlo'. Wells, who rented No. 86 Fort Road, Newhaven, in 1891, actually pulled off this amazing feat no fewer than three times. His luck didn't hold, however, and he died a pauper.

Though it was impossible to say whether shepherds' crowns were regarded as thunder bolts by the prehistoric and later peoples in whose graves examples were found, it was certain that the fossils were intentionally buried with the dead, and strongly suggested evidence of some cult or custom indicative of religious belief.

It was interesting to note, he said, that shepherds' crowns were picked up by practically every person working at Upper Bevendean and were either spat on and then thrown over the left shoulder for luck, or taken home to be placed on the window-sill. About 1875 these practices were widespread locally, because it was believed 'something dreadful' would happen if the crowns were not so dealt with. Such is the power of superstition, and some might say good riddance to it. Curator Toms made no such comment.

A bumper crop of crowns

In 1875, a Mr. Blackman, who lived in Caledonian Road, Brighton, was employed on Upper Bevendean Farm as a regular hand, and a principal job was hoeing crops. According to Toms, Blackman never passed a shepherds' crown when hoeing, but picked it up, religiously spat on it, and then cast it over his left shoulder for luck. This led to two brothers named Turvey playing a practical joke on Blackman.

Gathering a good number of crowns, they strewed them between the rows of the crop he was due to hoe on the following day, with the result that Blackman, in conformity with his invariable practice, was compelled to stoop and pick up each crown, to spit upon it and to throw it over his shoulder. Much to the amusement of the Turvey brothers, Blackman was later heard to remark that he had never seen so many crowns massed in one field.

Eggy oddity

On Ascension Day in Sussex an egg used to be hung on cottage roofs in order to protect their inhabitants from harm.

Fright for fisher folk

The sight of a woman in a white apron put such fear into Sussex fishermen that they would put off sailing until the following tide.

Dalmatian delight

It was considered good luck to see a brown-and-white Dalmatian dog, to find and take indoors a piece of coal, put a goat in with sheep, pick up a pin and live in a house surrounded by laurel bushes.

In January, 1931, Toms noted that some labourers of 'superior class' who kept shepherds' crowns on the mantelpiece to ward off evil spirits, had taken to blackleading them. They believed that unless the stones were industriously blackleaded once a week there would be trouble. If the weekly routine was forgotten, the poor housewife would, on remembering, get out of bed to blacklead the crowns in the middle of the night.

Previously, Toms had been told of a very old lady, a Mrs. Bishop, at Ham Manor, Angmering, who kept shepherds' crowns on her mantelpiece and regularly polished them with blacklead. Crowns were also considered lucky in the Selsey district, and here they were varnished before being placed on the mantelpiece.

SHEPHERDS' CROWNS AND WITCHSTONES

MR. TOMS' TALK TO WORTHING ARCHÆOLOGISTS

QUAINT FOLK-LORE

A talk on folk-lore and customs which have persisted even to the present day in the use of witchstones and shepherds' crowns, was given by Mr. H. S. Toms (curator of Brighton Museum) to members of the Worthing Archæological Society at the Art Gallery on Monday night.

A witchstone is an ordinary stone with a natural hole through it, and a shepherd's crown is a fossilised sea urchin. Both these potent charms are so ordinary as to be picked up frequently on the beach and on the hills, but they are not to be despised. They act against illness and witches, and bring good luck, the visitor stated.

News report in Worthing Herald, 13th November, 1930.

44

The man who loved lucky stones

Herbert Samuel Toms

Y ou may find it decidedly odd to learn that the man with undoubtedly the greatest passion for lucky stones of anyone anywhere was none other than the hard working, meticulous curator of the Brighton Museum in the twenties and thirties. He not only collected them but energetically hunted them down all over Sussex and beyond, and kept hundreds of detailed notes. When Herbert Samuel Toms retired after 40 years with the museum, he left a multitude of files, drawers and cabinets full of his observations and findings relating to prehistoric times in Sussex.

18th Feb 1928.
Barbican House, Lewes

Holed flint about this
size & shape, found
with

in Anglo Saxon Cemetery
at
Alfriston.

One of the many notes left by H.S. Toms. It reads '18th Feb 1928. Barbican House, Lewes. Holed flint about this size and shape, found with .... in Anglo Saxon cemetery at...... Alfriston.'

I was fortunate to be allowed access to one such cabinet and it is stuffed full of lucky stone lore. There are dates, names and addresses, minute details, even times, of his encounters with people who possessed lucky stones. He would stop strangers in the street and ask if they had seen or owned one. His sharp eyes could spot them from 200 yards away or more, and the following note is typical of the very many he left for posterity:

5th September, 1930.

When returning from Dorchester to Brighton in fast train, saw, when train was going at great speed, a lucky stone with pendant bunch of same hanging on shed south of railway at Lyndhurst Road, New Forest.

There are pictures and drawings in his cabinet of a whole range of stones and the places where he found them. The objects of his boundless curiosity were nailed to barn doors, hung over front doors, displayed on window-sills and tied to lucky horseshoes.

Sussex folk invited him into their homes to view stones on mantel-pieces, suspended from ceilings and tied to bed heads. People of all classes wrote to him, including a retired lieutenant colonel in Newhaven who swore he'd seen patients in a hospital in Baluchistan wearing lucky stones around their necks.

He gave lectures all over Sussex on a variety of subjects, including ponds and pond life, but his talks on lucky stones with all their underlying mystery and magic must have been most popular. His knowledge of Sussex archaeology was said to be unsurpassed, and he was indefatigable when some unusual item was unearthed and he was asked to travel to the spot to identify it.

We may wonder why such a scholarly man, deeply concerned with digs, ancient urns, old domestic utensils and neolithic burial sites, should have developed this love of lucky stones.

Picking up the daisies

The lovely little daisy has been prominent in Sussex life for many years. May queens were garlanded with them, and they figured decoratively in mid-summer floral festivals.

It was said to be lucky if you trod on the first daisy of the year, but if you allowed a young child to touch it, that was unlucky. If you were silly enough to uproot it, so the superstition went, your family would be stunted. If a young maiden wished to know how long she'd have to wait for marriage, she had to reach out with eyes closed and pick a bunch of daisies. When she counted them, each would represent a year. Some maidens must have preferred to pick larger flowers!

When talking to members of the Worthing Archaeological Society, he said he'd stumbled on the lore after seeing a holed stone hung on the point of a horseshoe outside a cottage. This instantly grabbed his attention. He followed it up, made more and more absorbing discoveries, and was soon investigating lucky stones all over the county.

He was 62 when he died. Such a short retirement for such a busy man with so much left to discover! They found him dead beneath a tree in the garden at the rear of the Greyhound Inn at Cocking Green. There was no inquest, so he must have died of natural causes. Even Toms' luck had to run out sometime.

It was December, 1940. The war was well under way, and the *Brighton Gazette,* running on rationed paper, had more to write about than the demise of the former curator of Brighton Museum, but it afforded him a fine obituary, detailing his painstaking thoroughness, interesting finds, lifetime of research work and 'unsurpassed knowledge' of Sussex archaeology.

Hidden passion

There was not a word about his passion for lucky stones, and the *Gazette* said this: 'For the greater part of 40 years he had been a virtual but willing "prisoner" in his quiet office in Brighton, poring over archaeological finds, examining ancient coins and ethnological specimens of all kinds which were taken to him for examination and advice.'

A prisoner? On the contrary, Herbert Toms appeared to roam freely throughout the county and beyond in his unceasing search for the stones that had become such an important part of his life.

Tell it to the bees

In Old Sussex people believed that bees had supernatural powers and that 'telling the bees' news of births, marriages and deaths would placate them. The Rev. William Parish, in his Dictionary of the Sussex Dialect, *says 'There is a superstition in the county, that if a piece of black crepe is not put round the hive after a death in the family, the bees will die.'*

Lillian Candlin, in Tales of Old Sussex, *tells of an East Sussex man whose father had died and who, on walking down the village street at East Dean, was asked if he had told his bees. 'No,' he said, 'I ain't. I've got enough to do without a telling of his bees.' His questioner replied 'If you had a told them I would have bought 'em, but they won't be no good now.' And they weren't - they all died.*

Bad luck!

That the former curator of Brighton Museum was a tidy, meticulous man there can be no doubt. One has only to examine his files and study his neatly typed and dated notes to be aware that he was a stickler for detail and a believer in direct action and follow-ups.

He was forever conducting interviews, collecting evidence and seeking confirmations. One might have thought him to be a stuffy, studious chap. Studious he undoubtedly was, but hardly stuffy, as his notes reveal. I have chuckled over many of them and wondered at his patience and the gullibility of some of his correspondents.

From among the many entries in his files I have copied a few of the more unusual ones. Of necessity, some have been shortened. I hope you will be as fascinated by them as my wife and I were.

H.S. Toms filed his notes under the following headings:

A. Beads and rosary.	**J. Curing ague.**
B. Drowning (boats and persons).	**K. Pocket.**
C. Vehicles, ploughs, lobster pots.	**L. Worn on person, inc. children.**
D. Keys.	**M. Handbag, perambulator etc.**
E. Spitting through or on.	**N. On trees.**
F. At doors and front garden.	**O. Miscellaneous.**
G. Window sills.	**P. Archaelogy and ethnology.**
H. Indoors. Including lightning.	**Q. Press notes.**
I. Stables, sheds etc.	**R. Stealing**

The index ends at 'R'. You may find some of the headings odd. Some of the contents are even odder.

LUCKY STONE AND HORSESHOE

Mrs. W. Ford, Thatched Cottage, Beddingham, Sussex.

Holed stone hung on the horseshoe by Mr. G. Banister. I observed 26th February, 1928. THIS WAS THE FIRST STONE I HAD SEEN HUNG IN SUSSEX! It is now in my possession.

Mrs. Ford also has a single shepherds' crown on her mantelpiece.

To H.S.Toms (he seldom seemed to use his Christian name) this must have been his most important picture because the juxtaposition of lucky stone and horseshoe sparked off an ever-widening interest which lasted for the rest of his life. Despite the fact that he had been sent stones by people and discussed their significance, this was his first actual 'face to face' encounter. Many more followed.

LUCKY STONE. WORN TO ENSURE GOOD HEALTH

20th September, 1927 Kingston-by-Sea, Sussex

Received from Mr. P.J. Mountney, a holed
pebble, about the size of a walnut, formerly worn
for many years on string round neck, under clothes,
by Mr. Walter Robinson, aged about 76, Kingston-by-
Sea.

It was given by Robinson to Mountney in return for
several favours. Robinson told Mountney that the
stone was worn to ensure good health, and that the
only occasion he regretted wearing it was when a
friend jocularly punched him on the chest, after
which he carried the resultant mark for days.
Robinson left Kingston-by-Sea in the Autumn of 1926.

ROSARY. WORN NEAREST HEART or HUNG IN HOUSE

26th April, 1930.   Denton

After taking photograph of stones hung at front door
for luck, questioned Mrs. A. Savage, 1 School
Cottage, Denton, near Newhaven, re rosaries. She,
a Roman Catholic, was wearing one round her neck
next the skin, and told me that if one were so worn,
or kept, or hung in house, the result would be that
one would never want.

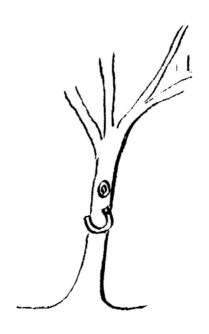

LUCKY STONE WITH HORSESHOE ON TREE

20th January, 1928   Clayton Holt, near Brighton

Informed by Mr. G.C.E. Goldsmith of Stanford Avenue,
Hassocks, that in the Spring of 1913 or 1914 he
observed fixed to the trunk of a tree, and about six
feet from the ground, a horseshoe with a lucky stone
above it in the south-east corner of Clayton Holt.
The stone was thin, about two or three inches in
diameter, with a large hole between centre and edge.
The stone was hung on a nail, but the horseshoe was
nailed to the tree.

According to Mr. Goldsmith's recollection, the tree
did not exceed 20 feet in height. On an adjacent
tree was a trespassers notice board. On my visit in
1928, I found that the trees in S.E. Clayton Holt
are over fifty feet in height.

On hearing of another lucky stone plus horseshoe sighting in South Wiltshire, some months later, he picked up his camera and was off like a shot.

LUCKY STONE, HORSESHOE and HEEL PELT

Mrs. E. Coombes, Post Office, Tollard Royal, South Wiltshire.

Photographed 17th September, 1929 at 3.20 p.m.

Shoe and stone found and hung, for luck, by Mrs. Coombes, thirty years ago. Formerly hung outdoors on cottage, but now hung inside the house. The pelt hanging outdoors, with numerous horseshoes, on back wall of cottage.

Mrs Coombes says the correct way to hang horseshoe with lucky stone is as shown in the photo — the stone inside the shoe.

Heel pelt? It was used as a slipper to cover horses hooves and thus protect lawns or grassy areas from the imprint of horseshoes.

LUCKY STONE in bow of ROWING BOAT, for luck

The Brighton curator would travel anywhere to inspect lucky stones, and in 1929, after seeing one attached to a boat in Dorset a few months earlier, he was determined to find out more about it. So he dropped everything, and off he went.

29th September, 1929.   South Dorset.

Photographed in Lulworth Cove, South Dorset, the only holed pebble to be found in the boats beached in the Cove. It was securely fasted inside the bow with copper wire. I found that the boat belonged to Mr. James Charles, a fisherman, and interviewed him. He was interested to learn that, having seen the lucky stone in the boat the previous summer, I had come across to Dorset that day to photograph it. He said, 'Would you like to have the stone?' and, on my replying in the affirmative, he immediately exclaimed, 'No, I don't think that stone had better be taken out of the boat; something might happen.' I agreed, and supported his faith in the potency of the stone.

H.S.T. Note: LUCKY STONES are worn or fixed in boats WITH COPPER WIRE, as charms against drowning. I was told that COPPER, being a primitive metal, must be so employed in preference to iron or steel.

LUCKY STONES, holed flints, ATTACHED TO LOBSTER POTS

Letter from Mr.H.F.Horlock, Hillcrest Road, Newhaven

15th December, 1929

I have found out that the fishermen at Seaford and Newhaven used to attach the large holed flints to their lobster pots for luck, in preference to the plain ones. By so doing they generally reckoned to be lucky in their catches of lobsters. In my schoolboy days I actually remember them used here.

LUCKY STONES strung on beam of a PLOUGH

16th July, 1929   Upper Bevendean, Brighton

M.A.J. Turvey, 71 Cobden Road, Brighton, informed me that a Thomas Budgen, who lived in a little cottage where St. Luke's Church now stands, had a special standard plough on Upper Bevendean Farm, and to the beam of the plough he had strung a line of lucky stones. Both shepherds' crowns and lucky stones were also to be seen placed for luck on the window-sill of Budgen's cottage.

Lucky strike

In an address to the Brighton Natural History Society in January, 1940, H.S. Toms said shepherds' crowns had also been known by some as thunder bolts or thunder stones and were believed to protect houses from lightning, but the custom, which went back through the ages, was now rapidly disappearing:

'Authentic records which I have obtained from country folk well over 70 years of age, show that the lore was prevalent in the Brighton district up to about 50 years ago. But, even then, the fossils were very generally regarded merely as lucky stones which, if not brought home to be placed for luck, either inside the house or outside on the window-sill, were not to be disregarded when seen on the ground, but to be picked up, spat upon, and then thrown over the left shoulder as a sacrifice to the God of Luck.'

LUCKY CHARMS.   Grades of potency.   STEALING

13th August, 1936

An idea current among villagers and others in the South of England is that a lucky stone that has been given to one is more potent than that found by oneself. Also, that which brings most good fortune is a lucky stone that one has been able to steal.

Apparently, this latter idea is widespread, for Mr. T.J. Alldridge, in either his Sherbro and its Hinterland or A Transformed Colony refers to the natives as stealing charms to make them more effective.

Mentioning this to Major H. Blakiston, Chairman of the Booth Museum Sub-Committee, Brighton, on the 12th July, 1936, he said it was a common practice among the natives of Nigeria to steal charms, fetishes or ju-jus, and that such thefts had often caused serious tribal fights to regain possession of the stolen objects.

Footnote: In 1867 it was believed in Australia that a stolen horseshoe placed on the chimney-hearth would bring good luck to the house.

SHEPHERDS' CROWNS and LUCKY STONES

The Misses Bentley, Arundel Road, Poling, Sussex.

Photographed 18th August, 1929 11 a.m.

The crowns. were brought home by the Misses
Bentley's father, Mr. Stephen BentIey, about 50
years ago, 'for luck', and placed on the same sill.
Two holed stones were also brought home at the same
time, for luck, and placed on a sill in the
front door porch.

LUCKY NECKLACE of what seems to be Porosphaera globularis

Letter from Mr. H.F. Horlock, Hillcrest Road, Newhaven.

9th July, 1927

'In conversation with an old inhabitant of Newhaven, he informed me that as a boy he remembers seeing the daughter of a local fisherman wearing a necklace of natural holed flints. Her father used to pick them up on the beach, and he would not pass one by. The necklace was about three feet long, and consisted of from sixty to seventy "beads" ranging from the size of a marble to a walnut and nicely graded. This would be sixty or seventy years ago.'

LUCKY STONES, worn solitary or as a necklace as a charm against, or cure for, 'black throat'

10th April, 1930   Brighton.

Visited our former Irish charwoman, Mrs. Pearson, 8 Wakefield Road, Brighton, where her daughter Maud (who had previously told me of woman in Brighton formerly wearing a small holed pebble round the neck for good luck) informed me that she had recently interviewed an old lady from whom she had learnt that, many years ago, it was the custom among women in Brighton and other parts of Sussex, to wear round the neck, as a charm against, or cure for, 'black throat', one solitary holed bead-like pebble, or a necklace of the same.

SHEPHERDS' CROWNS on sill of Mr. G. Ruff, 134 Patching Street, Patching, near Worthing

Photographed 8th September, 1929. 1.45 p.m.

Mr. Ruff found the crowns in position when he took possession of the cottage in 1923. They were placed on the sill by a former occupant, Mr. G. Stanford (who now lives higher up the street) in about 1909.

Regarded by Ruff and Stanford as curiosities, but the custom is evidently a survival from the time (about 50 years ago) when nearly every local cottage sill had its full complement of crowns, which were regarded as lucky.

LUCKY STONE, throwing over head, seashore

From The Aquarium by P.H. Gosse   London, 1854

'Nor was this the only thing that reminded me of
early days. As I sauntered with downcast eyes over
the shingle, my eyes caught a perforated pebble, and
in an instant the rude distich of boyish days came
up to my recollection, and I involuntarily
repeated:

Lucky stone! lucky stone!
Go over my head,
And bring me some good luck,
Before I go to bed!

'For it was one of the superstitions of my
childhood, taught and believed by credulous school
fellows, that the boy who found such a perforated
stone, and threw it over his head with the above
doggerel rhyme, would not fail to reap a swift
harvest of luck. What a strange faculty is memory!
I had not thought of this rhyme and its associations
for perhaps thirty years, and yet the sight of the
pebble brings up the perfect recollection, as if it
had been only yesterday that I had played at canal
digging and boat sailing on the shore.'

LUCKY STONE worn for years and then buried with owner

9th October, 1927   Portslade

Mrs. A.E. Weller, Wichhurst Cottage, Fulking,
Sussex, gave me the interesting information that her
mother, Mrs. G. Moore, of Portslade, who died in
1918, had worn round her neck a very small brown
holed flint (not exceeding a marble in size) for
years, for luck, and that this pebble was buried in
the coffin with her mother.

AGUE STONES, holed beach pebbles, kept as a CURE FOR AGUE in the cottage window of the late Mrs. Woolgar, of Southease, Sussex, from before 1870 until her death in June, 1896.

The stones are in the possession of Mrs. Fred Moore, Mrs. Woolgar's daughter. Mrs. Moore, aged 62 years, lent the stones to H.S.T. for the purpose of photography, 20th October, 1929, and they were returned to her on the 26th October, 1929.

Photographed 22nd October, 1929, in diffused light of Room 13, Brighton Museum. f32/4 minutes.

One can almost gasp at H.S.T.'s details, until you remember that he was a trained archaeologist, and every scrap of information was important. Not only did he find time to keep his entries up to date, but he talked to people. Today's officials could learn much from him.

LUCKY STONES attached to keys in house

Upper Bevendean, Brighton

3rd March, 1929.

Was informed by Mr. E.W. Boniface, carter, Upper Bevendean, Brighton, that he had attached small holed flints to bunches of keys for luck, and that he had brought home and hung inside the house similar holed flint for luck.

LUCKY STONES tied to keys for luck, Brighton

1st August, 1929.

Interviewed on ploughed field north of Hollingbury, Mr. E. Galby, in 71st year, of 21 William Street, Brighton, who came to this district when three years old and has been here practically ever since. He informed me that he had kept a small holed flint tied to his bunch of keys for luck for many years, but had since given it away to a friend to bring him good luck.

LUCKY STONES spat through for luck, Brighton.

23rd April, 1927.

Mr. R. Brown, in Booth Museum, when shown holed stone, said that, when a lad, he and others used to pick up such flints on the downs, spit through the hole for luck, and then throw stone away over left shoulder. He had, too, frequently seen locally such holed lucky flints attached to bunches of stable keys.

HOLED FLINT PEBBLES (7 Lucky Stones)

Found with Romano-British pottery vessels on Lancing Down, Sussex, prior to 1894, and presented in that year to the Dorset County Museum by Colonel Bramble (ex Medhurst College).

Borrowed 2nd September,1930, and photographed near window of bedroom in hotel, Dorchester, 10.30 am f32/8 secs.

Toms probably took a poor view of these important relics being handed to a Dorset museum. They were, after all, found in Sussex and, because they were interred with Roman remains, provide positive evidence of the high regard for lucky stones in those early days.

LUCKY STONES hung in houses, Lewes

Spring of 1929.

On the way from Mary Farm to Falmer, walked with a telegraph messenger who had come over from Lewes. He told me that outside his home at Lewes they had several holed flint pebbles (from Brighton beach) and a similar pebble hung inside the house. The lad said the practice was common in Lewes.

LUCKY STONES. Spitting through holes for luck

9th May, 1927, in Brighton Museum.

Mr. T. Virgo, 5 Clayton Road, Brighton, said he remembered picking up holed flints, spitting through the hole, and then throwing away for luck. If such holed stones were found on the beach, they were spat through and then thrown into the water. This he remembers doing about 34 years ago.

HAG STONES hung at the bed's head and tied to stable keys

Mrs. Frances Grose, author of Provincial Glossary, says: 'A stone with a hole in it, hung at the bed's head, will prevent the nightmare: it is therefore called a hag stone, from that disorder which is occasioned by a hag or witch sitting on the stomach of the party afflicted. It also prevents witches riding horses, for which purpose it is often tied to a stable key.'

LUCKY STONE, spat on and thrown over head for luck

27th April, 1930. High Park Corner, near Standean.

Interviewed Mr. Thomas Lee (relative of Gypsy Lee, who knows some of the Romany language), gypsy caravan, High Park Corner. Lee works for Capt. Nickson, Standean.

He told me that when he picked up a holed stone, he first wished that the Lord would send him better luck, then spat on the stone, shut his eyes, and threw stone backwards over his head.

Mr. R. Page, the gypsy of Tanner's Pond, who was present, said that this custom of wishing, spitting on, and shutting eyes before throwing overhead, was widespread, and had been handed down through his forebears. The same ritual was gone through with a horseshoe. Page also remembered shepherds' crowns being taken home and placed on mantelpieces for luck.

LUCKY STONES. Spat through and cast into sea

2nd July, 1927.

Mr. P.J. Mountney, of Southwick, informed me that a Mr. Muggeridge, now aged about 85, of Southwick, used to collect 'blue stones' (flints washed blue by the waves) on the foreshore at Southwick many years ago, to sell to glass makers. Muggeridge had told him that 'it was a very lucky day when he found a flint boulder with a hole through it.'

When such a holed flint was found they spat through the hole and cast the flint into the sea.

LUCKY STONES for curing ague. Firle

31st October, 1926.

Mr. J. Pettitt, born 1861, of Upper Roedale, Brighton, informed me that he remembered a holed flint tied by his mother to the bedstead in order to cure his brother, who was down with the ague. This happened at Firle, about 1870.

LUCKY STONES for curing ague. Southease

13th October, 1929.

In converse with the Rev. W.W. Thomas, Southease, learnt that a Mrs. W. Woolgar (deceased in June 1896), kept a row of holed lucky stones inside her window for the cure of some disease. At the instance of the Rev. Thomas, interviewed the daughter of Mrs. Woolgar (Mrs Fred Moore, of Southease), who still has the stones (a string of eight or nine holed pebbles) which she said were kept by her mother for the cure of the ague and were known as 'ague stones'. Her mother had them for many years from about 1870 onwards. Mrs. Moore believes in the efficacy of the ague stones, and would not part with them.

LUCKY STONES to prevent nightmare (riding of horses by hags).

From Brand's Popular Antiquities. The author of Vulgar Errors tells us that hollow stones are hung up in the stables to prevent the nightmare (vis the hag from riding their horses). The flint thus hung does hinder it.

LUCKY STONES inside house. Firle

30th March 1930.

Interviewed Mr. Albert Jarman, a labourer over 60 years of age, who has occupied Tilton Hovel, about a mile south of Firle Beacon, and he informed me that, until recently, he had kept holed flints hung inside the hovel, which consists of one room, for luck. He knew nothing of the lore attached to shepherds' crowns though he knew the fossils. Jarman had nailed three horseshoes, points up, on his door.

LUCKY STONE, King and Queen Bar, Brighton

28th February, 1928.

W. Tettersell told me that, before the alterations some years ago, a lucky stone was hung up over the Australian wines in the bar of the King and Queen in Marlborough Place, Brighton.

LUCKY STONES on window-sills. Piddinghoe

13th October, 1929.

Mr. A.H. Turvey, 71 Cobden Road, Brighton, when I told him of my recent visit to Piddinghoe and Southease, informed me that, about 1870, there lived in two old cottages by the river, at the north end of Piddinghoe, two old women, who wore hoods, and that the sills of their cottages were crowded with shepherds' crowns and lucky stones.

LUCKY STONES spitting on for luck

2nd August, 1929.

Met in the street Mrs J.B. Hadlow, of 46 Rugby Road, Brighton, who told me that when she was a child, she, with other girls, used to search for holed pebbles on the Brighton beach, and having found one wished, spat on the stone, and threw it over the left shoulder for luck (realisation of wish).

LUCKY STONE. Kept in handbag. Brighton

31st January, 1930.

Called on Mrs. S. Hulse, 20 Wood Street, Brighton, to see 'Jack' the jackdaw which we gave to her husband, our old milkman, over nine years ago. Coming out, saw a bunch of horseshoes hung behind and on front door. Asked if she had any other luck charms, and she showed me a holed flint which she had found about a year ago and placed in her handbag for luck. Mrs. Hulse also showed me some holed odd coins informing me 'anything with a hole in it is lucky'.

LUCKY STONE carried in pocket. Brighton

21 June, 1926.

Mr. Ernest Male, public library, Brighton, informed me that his father, aged 80 when he died in December, 1920, carried a small, holed flint in his pocket, for luck, nearly all his life.

Mr. Male said that the lucky stone carried by his father was an ordinary flint, about the size of a cob nut, with a natural hole right through the centre.

Hard luck for some

*With luck, you can't have it all your own way.
You have to take the rough with the smooth,
the yin with the yang, and there were several
things Sussex folk considered most unlucky. It
was thought to be a bad omen if you saw a
Death's Head moth, if someone opened an
umbrella indoors, if you caught sight of a new
moon through glass or had a picture fall
without apparent cause.*

*Tough luck, too, if you came across a large
number of ladybirds, spilt salt or watched as a
bird flew into your house. As for glancing
over your left shoulder and seeing a magpie -
horror!*

*In this so-called enlightened age, you'd think
that superstitions were things of the past. Not a
bit of it. People still throw spilt salt over their
shoulders, cross their fingers, knock on wood
and refuse to walk under ladders.*

The Rottingdean wishing stone

'Built into the wall surrounding Rudyard Kipling's old house at Rottingdean is a lucky stone head. Anyone who strokes the nose gently in a clockwise motion with the forefinger of the right hand, then turns round three times, will be granted their dearest wish – or so local legend maintains.'

That short paragraph appeared in a book called *Folklore, Myths and Legends of Britain,* published by the Reader's Digest Association in 1973. I was working for BBC Radio Brighton at the time, and was sent a copy for favour of review. When I saw the mention of the wishing stone, I sat up. I am ever curious about such things and was once taught by a demanding editor to be on constant alert for the odd, unaccountable and unusual. I set out with my family to examine it, but after searching the entire outer garden wall of Kipling's house, The Elms, failed to find any trace of the stone.

Keeping witches away

Sussex folk were wary of the sweet smelling hawthorn, not just for its sharp prickles but because it was said to be protected by a woodland god. To bring it into your house before May Day was to court disaster.

On the other hand, if you had a rowan bush in your garden, you were more than lucky. Witches would keep well away and so would evil-doers. Today's electronic burglar alarms are so much more effective – and expensive!

In my review, which was broadcast live in a books programme, I castigated Reader's Digest for failing to properly check its stories, and concluded that the stone head might have existed in earlier years, but was no longer there.

To my surprise, once I'd left the studio, I had several calls from Rottingdean listeners awaiting me. All acknowledged that the stone head was hard to find, but it was, they insisted, very definitely there. All, without exception, claimed that it really did work. There were, however, four warnings. You should never wish for money, never reveal your wish, never mock the head and always follow the routine faithfully.

We returned to Rottingdean and found the head, as directed by the listeners, well above eye level and a short distance from a side gate into the grounds. We could now see why we had missed it at the first attempt. It was set high, and tended to merge into the flint stone surrounds. It was not a head, more a grotesque face, with a nose flattened by too many enthusiastic seekers of good fortune.

Now, here's the strange thing. Our wishes came true! We never discussed them, but we all agreed that in some form or other we'd received what we had asked for.

'Strange powers'

Then I discovered a lovely, lavishly illustrated little book by Henry Blyth called *Smugglers' Village, the Story of Rottingdean,* in which he mentions the wishing stone with a bit more detail. He calls it 'A little ancient and mysterious stone face that peers down at you puckishly from among the flints and pebbles. This is the wishing stone of Rottingdean and it has strange supernatural powers.'

Henry Blyth goes on to repeat the ritual of circling the nose then turning in front of it, but he insists that you must only wish occasionally, when your need is great, and never, ever wish for money.

Witches in disguise

Could you be unlucky enough to own a tabby which is a witch in disguise? There are lots of superstitions about cats, but don't laugh, not too many years ago there were those in Sussex who would refuse to carry out a conversation when pussy was near for fear it would learn their secrets and pass them on to others.

Cats were also thought to be able to forecast the weather. When they clawed the carpet or upholstery, windy weather was on the way. When a cat sneezed it was a sign of rain. If a cat sneezed near a bride-to-be on her wedding morning, a happy marriage was indicated.

Kipling's house – The Elms.

As for the stone itself: 'It came originally,' he writes, 'from the churchyard, where it was discovered amongst some rubble many years ago. At that time the wall of The Elms was being repaired and so the stone was added to it.'

There are variations to this account, as I have found for myself. The parish church of St. Margaret which faces the village green provides the setting for our story of the mysterious wishing stone. The church has stood there since Saxon days and worship on the spot probably goes back to even earlier times. When you step into Rottingdean the centuries seem to slip by. All around you are flint stone buildings which have been standing there since pre-Tudor times. Relics thousands of years old have been unearthed, and many may still remain buried.

Hags on nags

Ghostly horses figure prominently in Sussex folk lore, including one at St. Nicholas's churchyard in Brighton that is said to appear on dark nights. Horses were thought to be vulnerable to the antics of witches, who would 'hag-ride' them round the countryside at night and return them to their stables all sweaty and unfit for work in the morning.

Sussex farmers took a poor view of this and nailed hag stones (lucky stones) to their barn and stable doors, and hung brasses around their animals' necks to protect them.

The wishing stone at Rottingdean. It looks almost alien.

French invade village

One story records that in 1377 French pirates invaded the village, killing and pillaging. Many villagers fled with their children, seeking safety in the church. They were pursued by the French who set fire to the building, burning alive all who sheltered within its walls. A very dark deed. Work on fully restoring the church did not begin until 1856 and left in its wake a litter of old stones and rubble. It all took considerable time, effort and labour, and since it was decided to reinter old bones as well as memorials, even more bits and pieces were scattered.

Many years later, the story continues, two workmen were digging at the old site, when the spade of one struck an obstacle. When they reached into the earth they discovered a bizarre-looking stone head. It was unlike anything they had ever seen, and there must have been an

Hair of the dog

In the 19th Century if you were bitten by a dog there was a real fear you might get rabies and start foaming at the mouth. If you did fall victim there was little medicine could do to save you, so a lucky charm was used. You plucked some hair from the dog, fried it, attached it to some rosemary and bandaged it to the wound. Hence the saying 'The hair of the dog that bit you'.

The hair of the dog these days relates to the custom of attempting to cure a hangover by taking a drop of what did you no good at all on the previous evening.

animated discussion about what to do with it. Glancing across the road to the flint wall that surrounds The Elms, they saw a hole in the facing which appeared just big enough to house the head. That is where they took it, and that is where they put it, mortaring it firmly into place.

Perhaps the most likely story came from a very old Rottingdean resident, who died soon after telling it to me, and whose name I failed to note. He said the stone appeared in 1922 or 23. Two workmen were involved. One was busily repairing the wall and the other sifting through a pile of rubble close to the church. He picked up a strange looking stone which was flat on one side and had a face on the other. He carried it to his mate at the wall, who promply seized it and cemented it in position, but instead of leaving the flat side exposed, decided that the face looked better.

My informant, who said he had known the men involved personally, had no idea of the stone's origin and did not want to discuss its reputed powers, being scathing of people who dreamt up what he called 'potty myths'. He was very critical of local writers who 'wouldn't know the truth if they tried, and always got it wrong!' He was a somewhat irascible little man without much of a sense of humour.

My connection with the wishing head remains constant, and has extended over 25 years. Many friends and visitors have been taken there, and the stories that have resulted are well worth recording, but there remains the question of where the stone came from before it landed in the rubble or emerged from beneath the earth. No one has bothered to date it or match it with any figure of similar appearance. Is it Saxon, or was it brought here from a foreign land? Did it once form part of a memorial stone? With its pop eyes and flat face, it appears almost alien.

Here again, how the wishing legend began with all its ritual is anyone's guess. Different people have different ideas, and the full extent of its wishing power has never been assessed, if indeed it has any at all. The local library and small museum, only a few yards from where the head

Lucky buns

Hot Cross Buns, or Good Friday Buns as they were once called, remain a traditional treat. Today's supermarket varieties are poor-tasting when compared with those sold by the few remaining truly independent bakeries in the county, which still manage to put plenty of spice in their products.

In the days before the war, however, some buns were used for altogether different purposes than eating. Lillian Candlin in her book Memories of Old Sussex *says some villagers hung them outside their front doors to keep witches and evil spirits away. Sussex fishermen, she says, were known to carry buns in their pockets before setting sail. The belief was that no man could die from drowning if he carried a Good Friday Bun.*

A Good Friday Bun kept in your house was also capable of warding off whooping cough, which was a dreadful complaint among children until the vaccines appeared. Another odd belief was that if you kept a Good Friday Bun it would never go mouldy.

is situated, has very little in its files worth repeating but the staff there are very co-operative. There is almost an embarrassment on the part of some local historians to acknowledge its existence, although at some time in 1995 the head was moved a few feet and re-cemented into the wall and its surrounds were strengthened, so someone is looking after it. Sad to report, however, with so many people eager to rub its nose and make wishes come true, the old gargoyle's face is becoming decidedly flat. Like the Cheshire cat, its main features may soon fade away, leaving just a gruesome grin.

Eyed with respect

There is a somewhat frightening side to the stone. It does not like being mocked or insulted. The two events I am about to tell you were witnessed by groups of senior Commonwealth journalists who were on annual residential courses in Brighton.

 In the summer of 1982 the course included newsmen and women from Asia and Africa and included a lady doctor from Kenya and a student from Nigeria we called the African Queen. The latter was large and broad but walked with grace and was most articulate, especially when discussing women's rights and colonial misdeeds.

As with most courses, the group was given the grand tour of Sussex and introduced to local personalities, lucky stones and the wishing head. Upon arrival in Rottingdean, the lady doctor, who claimed to be psychic, eyed the head with great respect and interest. She had seen similar objects in other parts of the world, and some, she said, were very powerful *ju ju* indeed.

She performed the ritual slowly and perfectly, with eyes closed and intent look on her face. 'Ahhh!' she said when she'd finished twirling,'I've made my wish. Let's hope it comes true soon'. The others followed her, some hesitantly, but all eager to have a go.

Love me

Be nice to mice!

According to one fable it was unlucky to chase rats and mice out of a house in the middle of the night while people were sleeping. It was thought that some human souls had the shape of such creatures, and emerged from their owners' mouths at night to take exercise. If you chased one away, it was said, the owner would die.

Then came disaster. With the fire of defiance blazing in her eyes, the African Queen stepped forward. 'This is all superstitious nonsense,' she exclaimed, 'and I'm surprised at you (pointing an accusing finger at me) bringing us here!' She then advanced on the stone, LEFT finger poised, and proceeded to encircle its nose in an anti-clockwise direction. She turned round it front of it, also anti-clockwise, threw back her head to let loose a few incoherent but nasty sounding words and spat fiercely on the pavement immediately in front of the object in the wall. There was a hushed silence and we all looked at one another. The doctor was aghast. 'You've done it now!' she said, 'and I wouldn't be in your shoes for all the tea in China!'

It was hot, I was thirsty, and we'd been on our feet all morning. I turned in the direction of the Plough Inn followed by a senior instructor and one or two students who were by now licking their lips and probably trying to change the inner wish they'd made for a quick pint of local ale. We were half way there when an anguished cry rang out demanding our return. It was the doubting African Queen, and we found her spread eagled across the roadway holding up the traffic and making noises that were attracting the attention of passers by. One elderly lady was sure she'd broken her leg, or back. She insisted we should send for an ambulance at once. At that point our resident physician stepped forward and said, 'Don't worry, dear, I'm a doctor'. That was a relief.

She looked at the African Queen and was terribly scornful. 'I told you what would happen,' she said, 'and now you're suffering the consequences.' She made a careful examination and diagnosed a sprain or twisted ankle. Nothing serious, she said, but she'd have to go to hospital for a proper check. Meanwhile the prostrate student was blubbering away and the traffic was building up. It took four of us to carry her across the road to a bench, whilst a colleague made arrangements to take her to hospital.

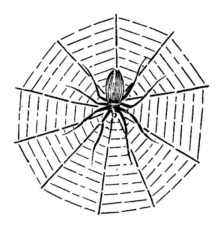

Spider charms

Lucky stones figured prominently in remedies for the ague in Sussex life a century ago, but there were also spider charms.

You'd probably try anything to offset the dreaded ague fever, even a spider rolled up in a cobweb and swallowed. Gulp! You could also apply it externally by placing the insect in a nutshell and wearing it round the neck in a bag of black silk.

What had happened was that she'd tripped on the kerb and all 20 stone or more of her had landed in a twisted heap on the tarmac. It was an unfortunate fall but she didn't receive much sympathy from her fellow students. As for the wishing head, it just looked on, and if it could have winked it would have.

In the following year we had a radio journalist from Peru with us. His name was Carlos, and he was a quiet, hard working, intent chap, but it was often difficult to know what he was thinking. Before we did our usual tour, we told the students what had happened when we'd last visited Rottingdean, and all promised to keep within the rules of the game. I also gave them a little talk about English superstitions, and told them that like the lucky stones these things should not be taken seriously, and were interesting leftovers from another age. All part of local colour, I said, and something to write home about.

Carlos made no comment. He'd been very quiet all morning and I sensed something was brewing inside him. We all lined up, Carlos insisting on going last. When his turn finally came, he drew himself up, and almost like a robot advanced towards the wall with his LEFT forefinger poised. We all groaned. Once again everything was done in reverse, and when he stepped back someone demanded 'Why?' 'Why?' said Carlos. 'I've done it to see what will happen next!'

Plenty of witnesses

What did happen was witnessed by us all. An hour later, he was taken ill with a high fever. He had to be taken back to the hall of residence and put to bed. The doctor who was called said, yes, it was some kind of fever but he didn't know which. He gave Carlos some medicine and said he'd call again. Carlos remained in bed for a week. On the seventh morning he woke up, felt fine, and resumed his studies. 'Sorry!' he said to us. 'I didn't mean to cause any trouble.' Perhaps he had more courage than the rest of us. He'd put the stone head to the test and the head had responded. But, of course, it could all have been a coincidence.

This is the Goldstone, pictured with the group of workers who had the task of first finding it and then digging it up. The date is 29th September, 1900, but it was not moved to its present resting place in Hove Park until 1906.

Giant of the Goldstone

It weighs more than 20 tons, does not have a hole through it, nor is it a fossil, but it is the biggest mystery stone of them all. It now sits in a flower bed in Hove Park, opposite what was once the Goldstone football ground, and an inscription close by reads: 'The Tolmen or Holy Stone of Druids. Col-chor or Godstone of Ancient Britons.'

How 'Godstone' became 'Goldstone' is not known, but it ranks high amongst the earliest evidence of human presence in the area. The rock is a greywether, of the kind used at Stonehenge, and according to the scant information available in Hove Museum it is believed to have been a focus of ancient ritual during the early Bronze Age, circa 2000 BC.

The stone stood for many years on farm land at Goldstone Bottom until about 1834, and was extremely popular. Archaeologists and large numbers of summer visitors used to go out to inspect the stone and wonder at its origins. William Marsh, the farmer who owned the land, was more concerned for his crops than ancient history and became so angry at the growing numbers of people tramping on to his field that he decided to bury it. The hole was at least twelve feet deep and it must have taken a lot of digging to swallow such a huge stone.

If the farmer had been angry, the indignation of locals and international experts alike was long and intense, but he was stubborn, and there was nothing they could do about it at that stage. The fact is that William Marsh was a prize chump. He could have dressed up the rock a little and charged people a tanner a look, and he would have been rich in next to no time!

This is how the sacred stone of the druids looks today. It stands in Hove Park in a flower bed, undisturbed by people or the passing traffic. Few know it's there!

It must be added that during the 1790s almost the whole of Hove was covered with a vast military camp under canvas, in readiness for the feared invasion of the French. Conditions in the camp were appalling. Many of the soldiers died of sickness and disease. In June,1795, men from the Oxford Militia mutinied, supposedly over the high price of bread. Edward Cook and Henry Parrish were court martialled and sentenced to be executed at Goldstone Bottom (near the sacred stone). The two prisoners were made to kneel at their coffins and the firing squad comprised men from their own regiment in order to drive home the example of their deaths.

Goldstone Bottom has been the scene of many terrible events, including whippings and other punishments. This was a sad, dark time in the history of the town. There is no mention in the records of lucky stones, or any lucky events at all at this time and place, but the giant Goldstone with its mysterious past was witness to it all.

It was not until the end of the 19th Century, when it was realised that Hove had an archaeological object of great interest buried in its bosom, that agitation grew for it to be brought to the surface. It took some searching for, and there was a considerable amount of digging involved, but it finally saw the sunlight again on 29th September, 1900, and was resited in Hove Park in 1906.

Today it is largely ignored. The traffic on the Old Shoreham Road hurtles by uncaringly, and few people are ever seen inspecting it. Modern druids appear to ignore it, but when Madeline and I last saw it, the stone was almost submerged beneath a mass of pink blossoms. A lucky sight, indeed!

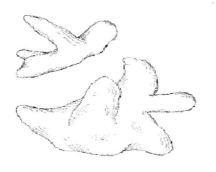

Above, typical flint nodules.
Below, this is what you see
when you slice through the
white chalky exterior.

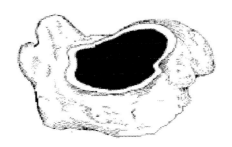

When you study the history and nature of flint you can only conclude that it is the most interesting rock of them all.

The luckiest place in the world

Flint arrow head

I t was a lucky day when I started my researches for this book because I was very quickly transported into the fascinating world of flint. Lucky stones apart, there is so much more to discover and learn about this mysterious rock. Mysterious it certainly is, with geologists still debating the chemistry that created it.

Lucky, too, when John Cooper, of the Booth Museum, advised me to read a book called *Flint - Its Origin, Properties and Uses*, by Walter Shepherd. Here is an author full of enthusiasm for flint, sparking off interesting facts and comments on almost every page, and providing essential reading for all caught up in the strangeness of the stuff.

As Walter Shepherd says, the nodules come in all sizes. Some are smaller than a grain of sand, others form blocks two or more feet across. 'They may be of almost any shape, from a perfectly round ball or a slender rod like a long finger, to an irregular agglomeration of assorted lumps, hollows and protuberances. They may be perforated with holes of any kind and form misshapen pipes, nozzles, funnels or doughnuts. Small specimens with holes were once threaded on a string

93

and hung on the key of an outer door, on a bed-post, or round the neck, to guard against witches and the evil eye. When so used they were known as hag-stones, but they might also be attached to a horse's collar as a charm against disease and children still call them lucky stones, even today.'

Well, we know all about the lucky aspect, don't we, but it is encouraging confirmation to have it repeated by an expert. Other flint nodules, he writes, are as hollow as a rubber ball and may contain smaller nodules loosely inside them, thus becoming 'rattle-stones'. Or the hollow may be lined with other minerals and sparkle with minute crystals when broken open.

Nothing like flint

In the early days, he says, there was nothing like flint, and man relied chiefly upon it for his very livelihood through twenty-five thousand generations. 'His food varied from day to day, but not his preoccupation with flint; the very evolution of his intelligence was guided by the contemplation and manipulation of flint — never a day could have passed through a hundred times the span of recorded history but the thought of flint crossed his mind or its image lay before his eyes.

'It may claim to have been of continuous economic importance for at least half a million years, and yet it is still something of a mystery. In modern times its nature and mode of occurrence have been intensively studied, but its formation is still not certainly understood. The origin of flint, so far as it is known, makes one of the most challenging stories in mineralogy, and it is all the more intriguing in that *finis* has not yet been put to it.'

Tempted though I am to quote more from this excellent book, I'll end it there and leave you to find Walter Shepherd for yourselves.

Perhaps it was the weird and wonderful shapes that attracted the early settlers in Sussex to flints. Whilst they were busy collecting them for manufacture into tools and weapons, they must have been struck by their two remarkable differences when compared with other rocks. They had strange shapes, and many had holes running through them, and it was the latter flints they probably put to one side for further inspection and discussion with their elders.

What has become clear to me is that way back in those neolithic days it must have seemed that the whole country was making tracks to Sussex. Many must have regarded it as the luckiest place in the world. Such was the unique nature of the terrain that the valuable flint lay buried there in abundance. It still does. Hundreds of mines were dug with great galleries leading off them. In a way, the products from these mines were more valuable than gold because they provided people with the tools to survive - tools to make more tools and tools with which to make cutting knives and arrow heads.

Evidence of extensive diggings was found near Findon, an area riddled with hundreds of deep shafts, some with galleries extending outwards. There was such industry in those early times in old Sussex, and when one examines the fruits of the flint knappers' labours on exhibition in many of the county's museums one cannot fail to be impressed by their skill and enterprise.

No, you can never escape from flint in Sussex. Buildings built with flint cobbles hundreds of years ago still stand, whilst much later brick dwellings and offices crumble. Flint in some form or other is used in the construction of our main roads and super highways.

Flint has provided us with a splendid legacy of luck!

Postscript

When the book was in its final stages two odd things happened, both at the same time and on the same spot.

The publisher had decided to take some close-ups of the Rottingdean wishing stone, and arrived with the author at the The Elms with great expectations, high quality camera and brand-new 36-exposure black and white film installed.

It was pouring with rain, however, and they had to choose the right moment to dash from their car, set up camera and confront the stone. All the preliminaries were ignored. There was no time for clockwise circles or upraised forefingers.

Just four shots were taken, and then to their astonishment there was a whirring sound from the camera as it proceeded to rewind itself back into its container. Any further picture taking was thus denied. An incredulous cry from David Arscott was quickly followed by a groan from John Behague as everything went silent. His hearing aid had ceased to function.

Pure coincidence? Or another reminder that the wishing stone requires ritual and respect? When processed the film revealed one good picture and three out of focus. The camera was inspected and found to be in perfect working order. There have been no further inexplicable rewinds and JB's hearing aid now has a new battery.

Perhaps it's time, though, that the local authorities installed a sign beneath the stone saying: PROCEED WITH CAUTION.